WHEN HOPE SPEAKS

Tara Payne

FOREWORD

This is the story of one woman's journey from excitement and joy to let down, disappointment and discouragement and back again. It is my testimony of years of silent sadness and solemnity to what I now experience, a life of joy that I attribute to having had the opportunity to become what I always wanted but didn't know if I would be able to be.

As I was going through this journey, I often felt isolated and alone. Unbeknownst to me, I met and was already in fellowship with other women who had also experienced miscarriage, but I had no clue. It wasn't until I became a mother that many began to share how they too had experienced this mystery.

When I became a mother, I vowed never to forget this walk and asked God to keep the feelings and sentiments fresh in my mind and my heart tender so that if I ever encountered someone else who walked this way, I would be able to comfort and encourage them. I promised myself and my Creator that I would share this account so that if you, my dear reader, or someone you know, found yourselves in this same situation, you would not feel alone like I did.

I would like to thank God for allowing me to make it through the very trying times I endured, to be able to write about my journey to motherhood and share it with you. My prayer is that you find the courage to hang on to any glimmer of hope you may receive by turning the pages of this book and know that the impossible is possible when you hold on to hope and move in faith.

Lovingly,

Tara

TABLE OF CONTENTS

INTRODUCTION

"He gives the barren woman a home,

making her the joyous mother of children.

Praise the LORD!"

Psalm 113:9

W hat is it about *not* being able to obtain something that makes you want it more? As a teenager, my mom told me that as a child, "nothing seemed difficult for you; if I put it in front of you, you did it, and you did it well." I remember being in an art class one blazing hot Oklahoma summer at a youth arts and humanities camp program in the mid-sized oil town where my sisters and I grew up. I noticed a magazine with a picture of a well-known local legend and began to put pencil to paper. What happened next blew my mind then and still does to this day.

I took a charcoal pencil and, glancing back and forth from the magazine cover to my drawing, made light strokes until it was complete. I don't remember if it was done in one sitting or if it took a few sessions or even days. The end result was upon comparing the two when I was finished even *I* was amazed. "You drew that?!" said my instructor. "Yes... ma'am, uh… I guess I did," I responded. I was in awe. I still don't remember when I learned to draw. It seemed to have just come naturally. I couldn't have been older than ten.

The same was true with music. Again, it takes my momma to tell the story correctly. All I remember is telling her I wanted to play the piano. She somehow got us tickets to a concert at the community center downtown where musical acts from across the globe went and still go to play. There I found myself, my mom looking on, in front of a baby grand piano, looking on as she struck up a conversation with a brown-skinned man in a black tuxedo, who knew a little something about playing the gargantuan instrument.

He sat down at the piano and played a song, and then he got up and asked me to sit down and play what I'd heard. So, I sat down, and my memory of the encounter is that I played everything he did minus a few notes here and there—so it was flawed in my opinion and nothing to write home about. Upon hearing my version, my mom quickly and *proudly* corrected me. "Don't you remember?" she asked, "You sat down and played the exact thing he'd played back to him." "I did?!" I replied. Wow. Really?! That still amazes me, but it's not surprising.

I was fearless and talented. I was naïve enough to assume life would be just like that—easy.

Having a baby wasn't easy. I had no problem conceiving. But carrying a pregnancy to term seemed to elude me. As a kid, nothing came hard for me. As an adult, God blessed me with great relationships (personal and professional) and a generous amount of favor through them, but this...*this* felt impossible.

"What do you mean, 'If I can'?" Jesus asked. "Anything is possible if a person believes."

Mark 9:23 (NLT)

Thinking again of my childhood, I remember being an artsy kind of gal. I drew and painted and danced and sang and imagined all types of creative concepts. I dreamed of becoming an internationally known vocalist who traveled the world and sang in front of thousands of people. I specifically recall an instance where I sang to all of the stuffed animals in my bedroom—a room shared with my youngest sister, Audra. She was such a neat and tidy person. I feel like my side of the room pretty much stayed a wreck. I laugh and roll my eyes simultaneously, thinking back on it. I wonder if her memory is similar. Anyway, as a girl, I remember playing with the popular toys and action figures of the day. But the first doll I remember buying with my own funds was a 'Disco Barbie.' She was Black, had a beautiful, shiny Afro, a long, sparkly, red gown and red high-heeled shoes. I was so happy to call her mine. We had other Barbie dolls too and played with them all often, but it gave me so much pride to have her because she looked like me.

When my sisters and I would play, we would pair our Barbies and our version of Ken (my Michael Jackson doll— complete with black loafers, a replica of his signature, red Thriller jacket, and silver glove). He was so dope! Of course, we didn't use that term back then. It may be outdated now, but who cares?

We had a blast pretending like the dolls were married and had a house and children. We would take turns letting our dolls be the mom and pair them with Michael Jackson, who was the dad. Those were good times! My little sister even had a Pee-wee Herman doll with a string in his back that you could pull to make him say a few of his famous signature phrases. Oh my gosh! She quite literally wore that doll *out*, pulling the string over and over again and laughing maniacally at the phrases, but probably more so at the annoyed reaction we all had by having to hear it repeatedly. My dad would take as much of it as he could until he felt he had to raise his voice and tell her to "stop that" to make it end. It was torture for us. Well, not real torture, but the kind you feel as a carefree child whose bratty sister won't stop doing something that annoys the life out of you. Yeah, those were good times. Playing with Cabbage Patch dolls, rocking and feeding them, and even taking them on family vacations—all the stuff little girls do. We didn't have a care in the world.

I strolled back through those memories because I didn't think a lot about the future as a child. I was having so much fun in the present. Don't get me wrong; I did imagine myself getting married and having babies. I wanted multicolored ones that reflected the skin tones of all my Cabbage Patch dolls. Of course, I didn't know how you had babies or even who I would marry. I think I just assumed it would be easy, like everything else, a fairytale that just happens. Back then, to me, a fairytale was a story of ease, beauty, fortune, and all good things—not bad. A fairytale doesn't have the same meaning to me today, but I still consider my life a fairytale.

As a child, I feel it's easy to see the happy parts of the story. As an adult, I see the challenges and struggles the main character(s) have to overcome, which is more like real life. I figured that being a mother would be filled with eagerness, excitement, and joy. Never did I imagine that my journey to motherhood would be paved with anger, comparison, doubt, disappointment, and even feelings of depression. But it did. I now realize all of it made me the woman, the mother, I am today. Being a mom has reconnected me to the gritty, get in your face, little girl I had inside that I had forgotten. If you are ready, I'd like to share my story, the journey to birthing hope, with you.

DISCLAIMER

The information in this book is accurate to the best of my recollection. It has been nearly ten years since the beginning of my journey. The words and sentiments contained therein are unscripted and the emotions raw—they are purely mine—right or wrong. The accounts of others, as needed, were given and used with full permission. No names have been changed. Any likeness or similarity is purely arbitrary. The story is mine, but it may also be yours.

CHAPTER 1 - BIRTHING HOPE

"For I know the plans I have for you," declares the Lord, "plans

to prosper you and not to harm you, plans to give you hope and a

future." Jeremiah 29:11

onday, January 18th of the year 2016 was a life-changing day in my life and in our household. It was a bitterly cold day; Martin Luther King Jr. Day. I remember the events oh-so-well. It was the day we birthed hope. Remember that word.

It was about 3:00 am, and I was thirty-seven weeks pregnant with our first child when I felt the urge to use the bathroom. I rolled out of bed and sleepily entered the bathroom. My husband was working nights, so I was home alone with our dog. I sat down sleepily and used the bathroom. I felt a strange sensation, followed by what felt like water gushing out like a faucet turned on high. "Hmm," I thought. "That was weird." It woke me up. After I washed my hands, I shuffled back to my bedroom to look for my cell phone.

After I googled, "What happens when your water breaks?" I discovered what I thought was a routine middle-of-the-night sleep driven trek to the bathroom turned out to be my water breaking. I determined I should call my husband, Anthony, who was at work, to let him know.

It was about 3:30 am by then. I called, very calm (from his later account), and said something like, "Hey baby... don't be alarmed, but I think my water just broke." His shift was set to end in about thirty more minutes, so I encouraged him to work the rest of it. I told him I would see him when he got home. I sat there in the bed, thinking, "What if this is it?" Partially nervous and partially excited, I jumped in the shower, still bewildered as to what was happening. I squeezed the shower gel into my bath pouf, scrubbed lightly, and slowly rinsed and stood in the shower. I opened the curtain and noticed the mirror covered in steam. I grabbed my towel and exited the shower. I looked back down at my phone and glanced back up at the mirror. I reached up to my left, grabbed a dry erase pen, wiped the mirror with my hand, dried it with a paper towel, and began to write. This is what it read: "3:05 am, water broke?" Just as calm as I had entered, I headed back to our room, got dressed and made sure my hospital bag was ready. Once Anthony came home and got his bag ready, off to the hospital we went. This is it. This is the moment I had been praying for. I asked God to perform a miraculous birth somehow and allow me to forgo labor, but I guess He decided against that. This was uncharted territory but somehow I remained calm.

We drove the cold, dark, empty streets to the hospital, which was about fifteen minutes away from our house. Upon arriving at the hospital, we checked in at the desk and informed the attendant that I thought my water had broken. They asked the routine check-in questions, asked for my insurance and identification, and handed me a clipboard of papers to fill out. Everything was very routine and smooth, and I was still feeling a strong sense of calm. So calm that my exhausted husband asked me, "Are you ok? Do you need anything?"

"No," I answered softly. "I'm good." I completed the paperwork, returned it to the desk, and sat as instructed until they called me back up to place me into a room. There we stayed while we waited for someone to come and check my cervix. I laid on the bed, and my husband sat, slightly slumped, in the chair adjacent to the bed. There he dozed off.

After determining that my water had broken and that I *was* in labor, they admitted me. They then transferred us to a different room where the great scene began. I experienced a fairly uneventful labor.

Inspired by a book entitled Supernatural Birth, my friend forwarded me, I'd been praying and believing that I could have our daughter naturally. I'd made up in my mind that I would not receive an epidural. The stronger my contractions grew, the more uncomfortable I felt. I had declined the epidural the last visit the nurse made it to my room. When she entered the room this time, she looked at my face and then the monitor and began to come closer to me. She let me know that I was about to get to the point of no return in my effacement and that if I declined the epidural now, and then later asked for it, I could risk not getting it due to safety concerns. She assured me that my birth would be no less natural if I took the epidural. I agreed to accept it. The pain continued to increase, and I didn't know if I could stand for it to get much stronger. I had only dilated to a four. From the stories I'd heard of other people's births, I didn't want to risk having to endure too much pain or struggling through the 'ring of fire.' She ordered the epidural, and we went back to waiting. By this time, some of the members of my immediate family had begun to show up. I'm not sure who arrived first, but eventually, my mom, dad, and older sister were all in the room with us. It was a holiday, so everyone but my younger sister, who works for a bank, was off work. We were all so excited. We had been waiting for years for this moment.

A little while later, there was a knock at the door. "Come in," we said. A man with strawberry blonde hair and a pleasant smile entered the room and informed us he was the anesthesiologist. He administered the epidural and then left the room. Not too long after he left, the nurse came in to check on me. "How are you feeling?" I hadn't told anyone else, but I felt like the room was getting further and further away and my hearing was fading. Everyone sounded like they were in a tunnel. So I asked the nurse if it was normal. She took a look at the monitor and looked back at me. "Uh oh." My blood pressure was dropping, likely in response to the anesthesia. She quickly administered epinephrine, and I felt the room returning back to normal. Not too long after that, I felt it again. She turned to the monitor again and then back to me. "Do you work in the medical field?" she asked. "Yes. Why do you ask?" I replied. "People in the medical field are always trying to take control of the room; worst patients ever. You guys don't know how to relax." We laughed in concert as I admitted I am a Type A personality. "We've got everything under control here. You just relax," she said. I can't quite remember when my doctor entered the scene, but there was talk of him possibly being stuck at another birth and not being able to deliver our daughter. That made me uncomfortable. After having most of my visits with him, I wanted him to be in the room with us. So I said a quick prayer (to go with all of the other prayers I'd prayed that *he*— and no one else—would deliver her). Thankfully, when it was time to push, about eleven hours after we arrived, in walked our doctor, bright-eyed, smiling, and ready to go. I felt a wave of relief. He shook my husband's hand and turned to me and asked if I was ready to have a baby. "I guess," I responded. "Whether I'm ready or not, it's time, right?" I chuckled. My dad decided a little earlier to exit the room, probably for privacy's sake, but my mom and my older sister remained until the doctor asked one of them to leave. My older sister left. My mother stayed. This would be her first granddaughter, and she was not going to miss it. She turned worship music on her phone and began to sing and dance, thanking God in advance for the miracle He was about to perform. The closer we got to our baby's arrival, the louder the music got. "Momma!" I exclaimed. "What?" she asked. "This is a celebration! We are giving God praise for what He is doing!"

"Yes, but can you praise a little quieter!" I asserted. She laughed snidely and rolled her eyes. She decreased the volume, albeit slightly, and continued with her personal praise party.

Don't get me wrong. I love to praise and sing and dance—I am on the worship team at church—but that day, the *last* thing I wanted to hear, so close to my ear, was loud, fast music of any sort. In my mind, when I gave birth, the atmosphere would be calm but worshipful, with the aroma of jasmine or lavender and oranges floating through the air.

I imagined the lights turned down to set the mood—like a spiritual spa, you know? Yeah RIGHT! Well, that didn't happen. "Ugh. Today is *MY* day," I thought to myself. However, because I didn't want to be rebuked or reprimanded in front of my doctor and the birthing team, I digressed. I let out a brief laugh and continued to push. Even at thirty-eight years old, she still evoked the fear of God. Not even an hour later, our little five pounds, nine-ounce baby girl, Asha Elise, was resting safely in our arms. As tears of joy rolled down my face, I paused to give thanks. Hope had arrived.

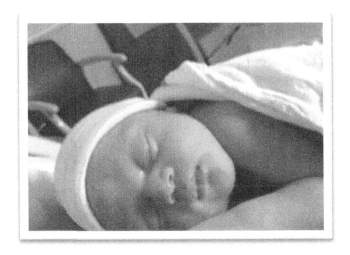

Our daughter the day she was born, three short hours after

delivery.

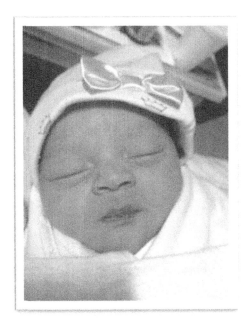

Later that same evening.

CHAPTER 2 - HOPE DEFERRED

"Hope deferred makes the heart sick,

but a longing fulfilled is a tree of life."

Proverbs 13:12

It all started in April or May of 2008. Anthony and I were newlyweds, and we were getting our passport pictures taken, at a local drug store, in preparation for our first visit to Canada for my only brother's wedding, in June of that year.

I was so ecstatic to go see my brother and meet his wife to be. She was a gorgeous Haitian-Canadian gem who he'd met while living and working in Chicago. The wedding and her family were beautiful. I was honored to be able to attend. I told my husband how important it was to me that I make it to this wedding. We had a delightful time. It was unlike anything I'd ever experienced. He didn't mention it then, but my husband said that he had a feeling we were going to get pregnant on the trip. Not long after we returned home, my cycle was late. So, we took a pregnancy test (or two or three) and learned that I was with child.

How surprised we were; I was. It felt like my husband wasn't as excited. I was so excited that I spoke to my husband about how to share it with his mom. He was her only child, and she wanted grandchildren so badly. I was proud to be able to provide them for her. When Anthony and I talked about sharing the news, he didn't seem as excited as I was to share. "I think we should wait," he said. "It's still really early." I think I was about four or five weeks pregnant, which is *really* early. I was so eager for my mother-in-law to know that I couldn't hold the news any longer. He was right but I was unrelenting, so he gave a nod of reluctant agreement but still cautioned that he thought it was too early to tell anyone. But you know how it is when a woman makes their mind up to do something. He probably knew I wasn't going to let up, and even if he said no, I might have done it anyway. So, I returned to the same local drug store chain, where we had our passport pictures made, and had a photo card made with one of the pictures we'd taken in Ottawa. So that we could give it to his mom to announce she would soon be a grandmother. Boy, was she beaming with pride when we gave her the card. I don't know how he knew, but very soon after we'd given her the card, we had a visit with my doctor and learned we would not be having a baby after all.

I was crushed, and I didn't understand what the doctor meant when he asked me, "Do you feel pregnant?" The question seemed dumb, insensitive, and rude. How would I know? I had never been pregnant before. Although now that I think of it, the nagging nausea I'd been feeling had gone away a few days before the doctor visit, but I didn't know what to think. I was just glad it was gone. It was so bothersome, and the only way I could get rid of it was to eat crackers and drink soda-ginger ale to be exact. I felt let down. It seems like as soon as we began to ride the high of it all, everything came crashing down. It was so heartbreaking, and the doctor seemed so insensitive and crass through it all.

He told me he was sending me for some tests. At our follow-up appointment, he revealed that what we'd experienced wasn't a pregnancy at all. It was something called a molar pregnancy. "A mole-Uh what?!" I thought. He explained and asked if I had questions. I said no and my visit was over. So was my pregnancy. And I began making weekly visits to the lab near his office to have my hormone levels checked to make sure they were decreasing as expected. If not, he informed me, I may have to go in for surgery. It took what felt like an eternity to me, and too many visits, but the readings returned to normal (not pregnant levels), and we attempted to return to life as usual.

As time went on, we managed to get somewhat past the loss (because you never get over it). We learned about a year or two later that I was pregnant again. Taking a note from what we'd already experienced, I heeded my husband's previous counsel, and we kept the news to ourselves.

It was good that we did. We learned in our first trimester, at around six weeks, that there was no heartbeat. I was saddened and stunned. "What's going on?" I thought. "What's wrong with me?" Disbelief filled my mind, and tears filled my eyes. The tears fell down my cheek and into the corner of my mouth. As I tasted the saltiness, I felt the sting of disappointment and rejection. I had so many questions for my doctor, for myself and for God. And it seemed like no one had answers. People said it was the body's way of showing that something was wrong and rectifying it early. I know they said it out of comfort, but it was everything but comforting. I was angry. Why was this happening to me? It wasn't fair. I felt a strange and eerie but familiar emotion wash over me. It was disappointment, and I was starting to expect it to show up every time I tried to break free. Is this how it's going to be? Though I am not usually quick to give up, I told myself in order to avoid meeting this fate again; maybe I should just leave it alone.

I had to decide if I wanted to let the pregnancy eliminate itself, or help it along with a D and C procedure, which is a procedure that

cleans out your womb by removing tissue from inside your uterus.[1]
After speaking with the doctor, I decided that having the procedure
was best, just in case my body did not eliminate it naturally—which
was a possibility. On the morning of the procedure, one of our friends
from church was also there in the waiting room. He is like an older
brother to me. I am not sure how my face looked when my eyes met
his, but I was instantly surprised and ready to run away. He didn't
know why I was there, and I didn't know why he was there. We kept
it that way. I believe we greeted each other. I may have even hugged
him. I'm not sure. I wanted so badly to say something to him, about
why we were there, but I didn't know what to say. I was really hoping
I didn't see anyone I knew, and I didn't want to invade his privacy
either. I went to the area, where my mom sat, waiting for my husband
to return from parking the car. There we sat until I was called back for
surgery. He never asked me what I was doing, and I never asked him.
We never spoke of it until years later when I was asked to share a
personal testimony about a cross I felt I had borne in my life, and how

[1] https://www.mayoclinic.org/tests-procedures/dilation-and-curet-
tage/about/pac-20384910

God helped me through it.

I felt like such a failure as a woman. How could having a baby be so hard? If I wasn't going to be a mom, then what was I going to do? I thought this was the natural order of things. You get married, and then you have babies. First comes love, then comes marriage, and then comes baby in a baby carriage. Isn't that how the childhood song went? "That's how it is supposed to be," I thought. I didn't even know *mis*carriage was an option. That wasn't even a part of the song. And I'm not supposed to be going through this.

As I lay there in a light blue gown, on a flat hospital bed, in a cold room covered in warmed but paper-thin blankets and preparing to go back to have this procedure, I thought to myself, "What happened? If I can do anything why is THIS hard?"

I have to pause here and say that after I came home from college, I never thought of getting married or having children. I didn't really have a desire to. In college, at the age of eighteen, I met and dated my first boyfriend. It was confusing, dramatic and tumultuous. Navigating teenage emotions and rationale was not easy. Though I felt he and I were in love—whatever that means at that age—by the end of our relationship, I was done with him and relationships in general. And I no longer desired marriage. I had tried so hard to become what I thought a good girlfriend was supposed to be that I lost myself and my virginity in the process. A whole army of emotions flooded my being, and interesting thoughts came with them. I rationalized to myself that I must've been missing something or not meeting expectations, so I went out on a quest to find out what it was. This is why I feel it is so important to have "the talk" with your kids, male and female, before you think they are ready. I left my poor little nineteen-year-old self bruised and maimed emotionally and mentally. I couldn't remember who I was or what I wanted or liked. Who could concentrate on school with all of that going on? I eventually dropped out of college at the University of Oklahoma and returned home to work and attend school at the local community college. That was one of the best things that ever happened to me. I began to re-learn who I was and what I wanted to do with my life. Later I returned to college only to once again earn academic probation. Upon my final return home, I began working at the local office of a national

Telecommunications company and moved back home.

Through one of my coworkers, who became a friend, I met a sweet lady who was starting a church with her husband. I began attending. I ended up staying for seven years. I learned so much about myself and God and life while I was at that church. Things that are foundational to the faith I have today. It wasn't a perfect experience by any means, but it was so eye-opening. It was my personal awakening. It was there that I was reacquainted with my love for singing and realized I had a gift and calling for worship.

Galvanized by encouragement from my sister I moved out of my parents' house, and into an apartment with my younger sister. We also worked and went to church together. One day, when I was in my mid-twenties, I found myself in my bedroom, in the apartment we shared praying in the Holy Spirit about my life. If you are unfamiliar with this vernacular it means to speak in a series of babblings that you cannot decode or understand, but God can (see Acts 2). It was during this prayer that I asked God to send me a husband who loved me like Christ loved the church. Almost immediately, I stopped. It was like someone else was praying and I was agreeing until I realized what was said. "Wait,"... I thought..."Did I just pray that?" Hmm, I pondered. Why would I do that? I didn't want to get married. Or did I?

While working at that telecommunications company, I met the man who would become my husband. We were introduced by a mutual friend who he'd grown up going to church with. She and I worked there together, and she asked if she could introduce me to someone. We were supposed to go to a sporting event, but somehow that never happened. I told her I would agree to meet him, but I wasn't looking for a relationship. I was quite content where I was, in my singleness. "You don't have to marry him," she joked. "Don't worry," I responded, "I won't." We met and began talking regularly. We soon became an item. Then, fear took over me. I didn't know how to be myself in a relationship without losing myself like I'd done previously, so I brought everything to a halt. He learned he'd gotten a job in another city in the state, and he called me and asked what my intentions were for our relationship. I told him we should call it off. He said ok and he moved away.

I continued my life until one day my mom and I were having a conversation where she asked about him. I told her we didn't talk anymore, and she began to probe, trying to figure out what happened. When I revealed that nothing happened, that I just wasn't used to a guy pursuing me and something had to be wrong with him, she said, "Something has to be wrong with *you*. You mean to tell me he was respectful and nice and liked you, and you told him *not* to call you? That doesn't make any sense, Tara. You should call him." So, I did. He was very surprised to hear from me and admitted, when he'd left the city where we now live to move to the big city, he'd purposely left everything behind, including me, because I 'd told him I wasn't interested.

We began talking a lot more. The cities we lived in were only about an hour and twenty minutes apart, so we found ourselves driving to visit one another. He met my parents for the first time while vising me, at my oldest half-sister's wedding. Upon introducing him, my dad looked him up and down (like I assume every dad would do) and said, "Who are you?" I said, "This is Anthony." "Who's Anthony?" he asked. "Daddy!" I said. "He's my friend." "Hmph. Nice to meet you." And he returned to what he was doing. As time went on, Anthony and I would spend more and more time together. He accompanied me to church a few times. He knew it was important for me to be with someone who had a similar belief system. Though the church I attended was a bit different than where he grew up (and frankly, it was different from the church I grew up in), he would sometimes join me. My family began seeing him more and more. I even went to visit him for days at a time, usually over a weekend, and went to church with him. Eventually, he moved back to Tulsa, and we became a couple.

On the day before Father's Day 2006, my family was having dinner at a local seafood restaurant. A friend of mine had given birth to her first baby about a month prior, and I wanted to go visit them in the hospital since they'd asked me to be her godmother and I hadn't seen her yet. During my visit, the baby spat up on me. I called and let Anthony know I had to go buy another shirt and we would be late meeting my parents. He insisted we drive separate cars and he would meet me there because he didn't want to be late. I'll be honest. I was a little perturbed. The first time I met his grandmother, she told me he had a tendency to run late to things. And she was right. I couldn't understand why it was so important for him to be on time that day. I was so annoyed at trying to decide if I wanted to buy a shirt or not that I just hung up and said, "Whatever." I went to Target across the street from the restaurant and picked up a shirt after debating in my mind if I should or not. "It's just dinner," I thought. But Anthony insisted I buy a new shirt and hurry to dinner. When I got to dinner, I was mad. The day wasn't going as I'd hoped, and I couldn't understand for the life of me why it was so important for him to be on time. I was baffled and bothered. After we ate, my mom asked me if I wanted dessert. I quickly and emphatically said no. I thought it was strange, but I agreed to go ahead and have dessert. As the waitress brought out the piece of Key lime pie we'd ordered, I looked up and noticed there was a box on top of the pie with a light inside. Immediately I thought whoa! Is that a...just about then I look over and at him and he is getting down on one knee. He nervously asked me if I would take this journey through life with him, and as my family is looking on, most of them in tears, I shrug my shoulders and say yes. That's why he wanted to be on time. We were married four months later in an outdoor wedding on a beautiful and unseasonably warm and sunny October day. The morning started off with showers. I was so nervous that it was going to rain on our day and that it would be bad luck for our marriage. Thankfully, the clouds gave way to sunshine, and all was dried up by the time we walked down the aisle at 5:30 that evening. In October of this year, we will celebrate thirteen years of marriage, and boy has it been a journey.

Anthony and I on our wedding day, just after being pronounced man and wife.

Let's fast forward about three or four years. We'd gotten married, had our first pregnancy loss, bought a house, moved in, and had another loss. I wish I would've done a better job of recording them and keeping track of the time, but it became hard to even think straight and not go into an emotional tailspin when pregnancy came to mind.

Some time passed, and we learned we were with child again. By this point, I decided that I wanted a new doctor. I had too many bad memories and one uncomfortable experience too many with the other one, so I went and asked around in search of another one. I wanted to try again to have a baby, but I didn't want to be reminded of my past failures every time I went to the doctor's office. And I didn't really feel like our personalities aligned. I feel it's important to be comfortable with your provider. They are viewing a very intimate part of you, and they should be easy to talk to and very informative as well as sensitive to your needs.

Since I'd lost two pregnancies, the news of another pregnancy struck fear in me. Almost immediately, I felt a panic rise inside. What if it happens again? I stopped allowing myself to be excited about hearing that news, and I began to let fear in. "At least if I endure another loss," I thought, "I won't have to be disappointed." It didn't help. I did experience another loss, and I was so disappointed that I literally felt like my heart had broken. By this time, I was bitter.

To clean out any tissue, my new doctor suggested I have another D and C. Our new doctor was a woman. Though I had never had a woman gynecologist, I was hopeful we would have a better experience with her. She was small in stature, soft-spoken, and personable. I felt she possessed the right amount of assertiveness and compassion. Upon one of my first visits, I reconnected with a friend I'd worked with as a teenager. She worked as my new provider's medical assistant, meaning she was going to be in the room when I had an exam. My initial reaction was…this is weird. But upon seeing her beautiful face and friendly smile, I felt like I had an ally. Maybe it was a sign, I thought. I had good feelings about her, so we stayed with this doctor for a few years.

After the procedure, I started to question God a lot. "Is it something I did? Is it something I didn't do? Is it something I said? Am I cursed? Maybe it's because Anthony and I weren't really meant to be, and you're trying to tell me something. Lord, why is this happening? Why won't you say anything? Why me? What am I supposed to do?" I went from questioning God to being upset with Him and avoiding speaking to Him altogether.

I remember sitting in the doctor's office waiting for an ultrasound, very early in my pregnancy, so early you couldn't even tell, watching an almost full-term woman and her family looking through a big purple bag the doctor had given her. It was a bag full of samples and tips for pregnant women. I know because I was given one at one time and then had it revoked when we discovered no heartbeat. It was just a stupid bag. At that moment, it was all that I wanted in the whole world. I felt that I was somehow shunned, and the purple bag became a symbol of a promise I didn't know if I would be fortunate enough to redeem. That pregnancy ended with a visit to the doctor not hearing a heartbeat.

"Here we go again," I said to myself. Now, I was pissed. Please excuse my language, but I was so angry I was beside myself. What the hell is going on? Maybe it's not God's will for me? I began to harbor a secret jealousy toward any woman who I saw with a pregnant belly or a child. It was strange because it wasn't a jealousy that caused me to want their child, but it was a jealousy that was steeped in insecurity. I felt like I was less than any woman who was able to conceive because I couldn't. And I didn't know if I ever would. I don't know if you've ever felt this way, but I was happy for the ladies who I witnessed being able to conceive and carry a pregnancy to term, but I wanted it for myself.

Time passed, and I was looking to get my hair braided. My usual stylist specialized in making her clients' natural hair healthy, but I wanted braids. She didn't do braids, but she was able to refer me to a woman she used for hers. I reached out to her to set an appointment, and on the day of my appointment, I nervously navigated, with help from the GPS on my phone, to her house. She was a very nice lady. She was from Africa, so she spoke with a beautifully thick, West African accent. She and her husband had come to Tulsa so he could go to a school for ministry. We talked about our lives and eventually began to talk about our beliefs. I quickly became comfortable talking to her. It was like we'd known each other before. I admired how knowledgeable she appeared about the Bible. She seemed to be resolute about her belief in its teachings and promises. We talked about almost everything. Quite naturally, our conversation switched to the topic of children, and I shared what I'd gone through. I shared that it must not be God's will for me to have children and expressed my deep-seated disappointment. She passionately, but lovingly, informed me I had the wrong understanding of God's view on childbirth. Lovingly, she corrected me and insisted that my statement was not founded in the truth of the Bible. "That's a lie from the pit of hell!" she exclaimed. "Childbirth is God's idea. Why would He create it and you for it and then say it's not His will for your life? That doesn't make any sense," she insisted.

I felt small, but I was a bit upset and embarrassed, too. I felt like I was at a point in my life where I was learning more about my faith, and I assumed that my failure to conceive and give birth could only be explained as not part of the plan I was programmed with. I couldn't quite understand how she could be so sure. Didn't she know that there were scores of women who wanted kids and couldn't have them? So... why, better yet, how could she speak with such assurance? How could I have a wrong view of this? Why haven't they been able to have a baby? She encouraged me to go back to the word of God and read it and believe it. She reminded me that it is written that "according to our faith be it unto us." That means we receive what we believe. I still didn't buy it totally because I didn't feel like it was fair. Before I left her house, we prayed together, and she asked God to show me in His word what I needed to see. I will never forget that encounter. I think about her to this day and the experience I had in her chair. Though I was not speaking to God, it was like He was making very deliberate attempts to speak to me and remind me that He was still there. Though I had given up on Him, He didn't let me go.

I'm so grateful that while I was trying to understand, reason, grieve and start anew, I could trust that the powers that be were working all around me, whispering sentiments of hope all along.

This has been a long road for me, and today, as I stand here, it's been almost eleven years since our first miscarriage, so some of the timing of all of my testimony may be out of whack. But I know we went through test after test, doctor visit after doctor visit searching for the reason why we kept enduring these losses and the doctors had no answers. I just read an article the other day that spoke of the mystery of the miscarriage. I wasn't interested in a mystery. I wanted answers, so I asked lots of questions. My questions resulted in a bunch of appointments to specialists and a battery of tests to try and determine the cause of our misfortune.

One of the first tests I had with the new doctor was a procedure called a hysterosalpingogram or HSG. Because I was in spelling bees as a child, I studied prefixes and suffixes and origins of words, and the sound of the full word is freakishly fascinating to me. *A* **hysterosalpingogram** *or HSG is an x-ray procedure used to see whether the fallopian tubes are patent (open) and if the inside of the uterus (uterine cavity) is normal. HSG is an outpatient procedure that usually takes less than 5 minutes to perform*[2]. As the definition explains, this test takes a look at your fallopian tubes to see if you have any blockages (such as scar tissue) that are preventing the egg from being released correctly down them.

Undergoing this test gave me such a weird sensation. It caused cramping, discomfort, slight bleeding, and it just felt *strange*. I don't know how else to put it. Emotionally and physically, I was uncomfortable. The thought of knowing my fallopian tubes could have been blocked brought back memories of all of the sins of my

---

[2] https://www.reproductivefacts.org/news-and-publications/patient-fact-sheets-and-booklets/documents/fact-sheets-and-info-booklets/hysterosalpingogram-hsg/

teenage years. Had I thought back then about possible future ramifications when I was trying to be a mom, I would have done a lot of things differently. This made me feel bad about myself and my previous choices of promiscuity and irresponsibility. On a positive note, it afforded me the opportunity to surrender those things and feelings to God, and I did.

Thankfully, the results came back normal. I felt a sense of relief, but I was still left with no explanation as to why I hadn't been able to carry a pregnancy past the first trimester. Upon receiving the results of the HSG, I probed about what else we could do. So, we were referred to a local fertility clinic to see if maybe there were genetic maladies that were causing a chromosomal discord or misfire of some sort and thus the failed pregnancies.

Being referred to the fertility specialist sparked an interesting conversation between my husband and I. We found ourselves discussing a method of conception I knew nothing about and had never even considered called IVF (in vitro fertilization). We were probably putting the cart before the horse discussing it, but my husband and I began to ask one another's feelings on exploring this method of conception. He said he would be willing to go through it, but I wasn't. Something deep down inside me, perhaps a divine stubbornness, made me feel like I was going to be able to conceive naturally, and I wasn't going to stop until I had my desired outcome. And something inside of me would not let me relent. I had a nagging sensation, or rather a dogged determination, within that somehow I was going to be able to have a baby without assistance (definitely no shun to those of you who may have gone that route or are going through treatments now. In my opinion, IVF is a miracle as well). I just felt like God was going to allow me to have my baby the way I had envisioned. After all the testing was complete, I had another appointment with the fertility specialist. It was interesting to learn that she had her own battle with infertility and had her child through something called IUI (intrauterine insemination). She explained to me that my eggs were in great shape and appeared very healthy. She said something to the effect of them being healthier than some of the eggs she has seen of clients who were ten years my junior and added that she wouldn't be surprised if I had a baby at forty-one. That was good news (kind of), but that still gave me nothing. Nothing. We kept coming up with nothing. And it was so frustrating. In essence, the results always seemed to conclude that there was no reason anatomically or physiologically why I shouldn't be able to have a full-term pregnancy. I began to hear over and over that it was a "mystery" and learned it was more common than I ever knew. Just the other day, I read an article by a woman who had coincidentally experienced four miscarriages just as I have. In it, she shared that "an estimated one in five pregnancies ends in miscarriage, with the majority occurring before the twelve-week mark. Seventy-one percent of people who lose a pregnancy aren't given a reason, according to a 2019 survey by the baby charity Tommy's[3]. You are told – repeatedly – that it's 'just bad luck', 'just one of those things', 'just nature's way.'" This mystery has left many men and women dumbfounded and offers no reason as to why these things happen. It can be so heartbreaking, but don't give up.

Here is an email I wrote to myself; a journal entry from what appears to be May 2014: *It's my birthday!*

---

[3] https://www.tommys.org/our-organisation/about-us/charity-news/tell-me-why-tommys-campaign

Yesterday we confirmed that you (two?) are in Mommy's tummy. I had been awaiting my monthly gift and each day as it failed to come I would pray for you and lay hands on my belly and speak the word of God over your life and my body. A few days I felt like it was going to come so I would confess the truth and promises of the Bible and it stayed away.

It all started with a dream...literally! A week and a half or more ago I dreamt that I was telling a woman (I don't know who it was, but it was clearly a feminine presence) that "this time it worked!" That THIS time I had felt the egg implanting and that I was pregnant. I remember being so excited! After that dream that's when I began praying for you and remembered that your Aunt Jonnel had forwarded me a book entitled *"Supernatural Childbirth"*. So, I started reading it again and boy it was so great! It gave me scriptures to stand on and even prayers to pray. I prayed them aloud but to myself and just yesterday morning at around one or two am I thanked God for you and that I would carry you to term; you would be healthy and bring joy to our family and walk in the ways of Our Lord.

So, yesterday, while your daddy was preparing the pizza and salad he'd brought home for dinner I took the test and as I took it spoke that it wasn't going to show a positive but that it would be positive.... As I heard myself say that I quickly changed my confession to "it WILL show a positive" and it did. And I was a little shocked but not really because I wholeheartedly believe what I'd been praying. So I went into the door of the kitchen and asked your daddy to come here for a second, and showed him the test was positive.

This is the best birthday ever because we have the joy of knowing you are on the way. I'm... We're so excited!!!!

CHAPTER 3 - FATHERING HOPE

"If you've been through miscarriage, others who have also been

through it will come across your path."   *-Anthony*

Some time after my mother-in-law passed, I thought to ask my husband how he felt about everything we'd endured. In my head, all of this was happening to *me*. I took it very personally. I wasn't trying to shut him out. I just felt like it was *my* failure, but I wasn't traveling this road alone. He had questions and he, too, was grieving. So, this chapter is to give you an inside look at what was going on in his mind, and may be going through your husband's mind—from my husband's point of view.

I feel that miscarriage is one of those things people don't talk about. I never knew there would be ups and downs or that we would experience challenges becoming parents the way we did. Pregnancy loss wasn't even on my mind, especially not more than once.

When we went to Canada, for your brother's wedding I told myself that we were going to get pregnant there and we did. Well, sort of. It turned out to be a molar pregnancy or a blighted ovum. I was devastated. Learning we were pregnant after coming back from celebrating the marriage of my now brother and sister-in-law, I remember being very excited. I was excited on our wedding day too, but I was more so overwhelmed that day, with all the details and people and things I had to do. It was a lot. Even though it was a lot, I wasn't the least bit nervous. I've always wanted a wife. I suspect, like most men, I just wanted to be married. Now, the wedding planning felt like much ado—colors and flowers, songs, food, tuxedos, shoes, photos, honeymoons. As men we just want to be official and have someone we can move through this life with. The wedding is mainly for you all as wives, but we do it because we love and want to be with you all. After we got married, I thought, this is it… very soon, we will be parents.

I felt like you were more excited about our first pregnancy than I was. I was excited, but I suspected you were more excited. When we found out we wouldn't be having a child at that time, I was disappointed and hurt. I was so proud when I would tell people, but for me to have to tell them my wife had a blighted ovum and I got blank stares in return.

We've had three doctors over this journey. Our first doctor was kind of quirky. Maybe he was a taste we weren't accustomed to. You had to have that D and C, and that bothered me after I found out what they were doing. I was so glad your mom was there. It was such a long day. You were so strong. You came out of the Operating Room like, "I am fine...I'll be ok," and I couldn't understand how you could say that. I thank God your mom showed me how to be more attentive to you. I felt sympathy and pain that you had to go through that. I couldn't imagine having to go through it. The shoe couldn't have been on the other foot.

In my mind, I wondered if it was something I did while you were pregnant or before you got pregnant to mess up the pregnancy process. I remember feeling upset with you one day when I felt like you did way too much physical activity. That pregnancy ended in miscarriage, but I never blamed you for losing the babies. I do recall us getting into a heated argument one day and I actually told you to stop aborting my babies. It wasn't until you told me that they weren't abortions per se they were involuntary dismissals, and the D and C's were to clean out any lingering tissue. I didn't really understand what was going on.

After the first doctor, we switched doctors. Our second doctor was nice. When we had to go through fertility testing downtown, it was disappointing because what I recall hearing that my sperm count wasn't high, and that was a blow to my pride. It was like they were saying my sperm wasn't strong enough to do what it needed to do in your body. The visits to the fertility clinic were weird, but I knew why we were doing it. But I was tired of the process at that point. I just felt like it wasn't supposed to be that tedious. It was hard, and I wish I knew why. It was different.

We found our last doctor through referral from one of my coworkers. I think we found him before we got pregnant again. I honestly didn't think you would go see him. I felt like a lot of times in our marriage you would reject me and my suggestions. So when you called, I was surprised. He was strange to me. I felt like I had to go to all of your appointments because there was something about him that made me uneasy. That's not the only reason I wanted to be there, but I didn't feel right letting you go alone.

In 2015, I remember sending you on the Girls' trip to North Carolina with your mom and two best friends. When you got back and told me your cycle was late, it wasn't alarming. It felt like you were always taking a pregnancy test. Then we found out that we were expecting for the fifth time.

Though you say you were nervous (during our fifth pregnancy), I felt like you were sure that this was a viable pregnancy. You had a lot of great and helpful input from your good friend, Lisa, that made me feel you were confident. As your stomach got bigger and bigger, I felt like it was getting real. I felt somewhat secure in this pregnancy because it seemed that every time you doubted, someone was always sent to encourage you. I will never forget one of our friends coming over when I was at work and being right here by your side when I couldn't. I was humbled and grateful because I felt like it was something I was supposed to be doing, and I was glad you didn't have to go through that alone.

Ohhh, baby—Boy or Girl??

The baby reveal was frustrating to me. It was overwhelming because I wanted to know immediately what we were having, but I didn't find out until the reveal because you wanted to make it a surprise. I regret doing that. The envelope from the doctor sat there for a couple of days, and I thought I could just open it. Maybe I was trying to consider you by not opening it, but I still wanted to know for myself...so I could process it a little better in my head. I struggled the day of the reveal because everything seemed like an overload having all of those people there. It was a bit much (a cake, all the people, etc.). Though I didn't want to go, I knew I was going. I was grateful for all the male support that was present in your dad and my friends, etc. and I'm glad I went. Having certain family members there made me feel good.

After the gender reveal, when we learned we were having a girl, I can't recall a particular feeling. Though I must've felt *something* because my cousin said the look on my face was priceless. I was just glad we really had a baby.

On the day you went into labor, I was excited. This was what we had been waiting for, and this was the day; after all the classes and all the appointments, this was finally it! Do you remember? You called me early in the morning...like 3:30 am. I'd worked the whole weekend, and after I got your call, I left work, came home to get you, and then we went straight to the hospital.

When I saw our daughter's head come out, I felt like I passed out in the delivery room, and I missed the whole thing. I wonder what that was about. It was before it was all over because when I came back to, and I still wanted to help with whatever the process was. I was so tired.

Having looked back at the whole journey—God is good. It was a hard road that I don't think I'll ever forget. Even now, when I hear of couples who are expecting, I have an unexplainable feeling like I hope to God they don't have to go through what we've gone through. I don't like trying to contain my excitement or holding it back. So, I just pray.

I think most guys sympathize with their wife for going through a miscarriage. If I could share advice with other expectant fathers who have been through miscarriage, I would say: Be the best expectant dad you can be. Ask your wife what she needs from you in the way of support. Go get the food they're craving, rub her feet or her back, or whatever it is that she desires. Personally, I was a little disappointed because I had heard stories of crazy cravings, and I was ready to go on midnight runs to satisfy your cravings, but you didn't have many cravings at all. You also weren't too good at telling me what you needed help with, but we made it through.

So to the dads, I would say stay in the moment. Don't try to go too far in the future—thinking about next time. Also, don't go too far in the past, trying to figure out why. Stay in the moment, especially if you want to have another kid. Don't check out. It's easy to do when you've been through all of that, but ... stay the course and stay supportive. Oh. Also, just a suggestion for the wives out there. I know going through this is not easy, and you can feel all alone. As a husband who has been through this, I want you to know your husband needs you not to isolate. Recently, I shared with my wife that I needed her not to get caught up in herself and forget that I lost a child too.

CHAPTER 4 - HOPE HAS FRIENDS

"As iron sharpens iron,

so one person sharpens another."

Proverbs 27:17

Picture this: it's May of 2015, and I'm preparing to go on a girls' trip to North Carolina with my mom and my two best friends. It was my gift from Anthony for me to go. Before I left, I wanted to make sure everything was right, so he wouldn't have to worry about what to eat, etc., so I made meals and made sure he was fulfilled physically before I left.

That morning, he drove my mom and me to the airport, and we

were off to meet my best friend for the first leg of my birthday trip. We flew into the airport in Raleigh/Durham. There we rented a car and drove to my best friend, Tori's place. It had been about five years since we'd seen each other in person. She had moved from Georgia to North Carolina for a job. Seeing her brought happy tears to both of our eyes. It was like the scene in the movie *The Color Purple* when Celie and Nettie were reunited after having been apart for so long. We met our first year in college and have been friends ever since. We lost touch for a few years but other than that have been in close contact and inseparable. After our embrace, we giggled like schoolgirls and began to catch up. We stayed the night there. The next day, we had breakfast, which my mom still raves about to this day (Tori makes the BEST grits—LORD!), and then drove to meet my other best friend, Nadège, at the hotel we secured in Charlotte.

We had such a great time that weekend. It was just what I needed. We shopped and ate great food and laughed and cried and laughed some more. One of the events that really made an impact on me was meeting Nadège's godmother. That morning, we met her at a country club near her home for brunch. Upon meeting her I knew I'd seen her before. I later discovered I attended a seminar she facilitated years before. Immediately following brunch, we followed her to her house where she had very sweetly set up a room in the back of her house so we could have a time of prayer and encouragement. It was a very pen room that overlooked her beautiful patio and backyard. When we arrived at her house, I visited the bathroom two or three times in the first fifteen minutes or so. "Girl," she said, "are you pregnant?" "Naw!" I said... thinking in the back of my mind, I could be but surely not.

While we were having fruit and muffins there, she prayed for each one of us individually and spoke a prophetic word over us. When she got to me, I felt like the lady in the Bible who said, "Come, see about a man who told me everything I ever did." She told me she saw me in the spirit, and it was like I got pregnant, and then it would go away and again and again. And she told me that she heard God say there was nothing physically wrong with me. "Your issue is a faith issue." So I look at my friend like, why you tell this lady all my business? And she looks back at me like, girl, I haven't said a word.

That trip changed me. I prayed and asked God, "What is she talking about? I know I have faith. I know you. Show me what she's talking about. What scripture do I need to read?" I kept asking. I kept seeking. I kept knocking. And I started reading a book that another friend of mine had given me a year prior called *Supernatural Childbirth*.

June of 2015, I found out I was in fact pregnant for the fifth time. Tempted to panic, I immediately went into prayer. I'd learned from the book that I had to constantly be feeding myself with the word so as to feed my faith and starve my doubts. The pregnancy wasn't without incident. I had an instance where I thought I would miscarry again, and I picked up my phone to call my doctor but realized there was nothing he could do... so at that point, I told God, "Lord, you're the only one who can get me and this baby through this safely." I knew that if I was going to give birth, I was reliant on God.

Picture from our 2015 Girls' trip to North Carolina.
These three ladies have prayed and carried me through alot of times.

All eight months and one week of my gestation, I was a praying, reading, decreeing, faithful, faith-filled, and faith-focused woman, and God made good on His promise. I, the woman who had endured four failed pregnancies, finally gave birth.

In the midst of it all—heartache, depression, doubt, fear, unbelief, hopelessness, anger, and even despair—He kept me. And I wanted to give up. Ok—let me be honest—I did give up, and more than once.

There was one day that I told God if He chose not to wake me up I'd be ok with that. I felt I had nothing to live for. I wanted to throw my faith, my marriage, and my life away. But He woke me up another day and another and kept me through all the hurt and pain. After having come through it all I can say I am glad He did. But in the middle of it I lost strength. I want you to know that because of the cross He carried, you can make it too. There is absolutely NOTHING He won't bring you through. Ask Him and believe. I'm not saying it's going to be easy, but God promised to be with us when we go through trials wherever they take us. As I sit typing this, I feel like it was all because I had to share this story, my journey, with you. And maybe, just *maybe,* someone who is struggling to be a mother will be encouraged.

So, our first meeting with our new provider was a little awkward because he had an unhindered, quirky sense of humor. He would ask you things like, well, someone had been getting it on. Though it was obviously true, I think both Anthony and I are both a bit guarded and conservative when it comes to talking about those types of issues. It made my husband very uncomfortable.

What I really liked about him was when I shared my history with him, he acknowledged my past hurts but didn't allow them to dictate what stance he would take as it related to the current pregnancy. He asked a couple of questions like, were there any reasons attached to the miscarriages? I told him we'd undergone testing but that the doctors hadn't discovered anything major. So, he proceeded like everything was going to be fine from day one. When I inquired about needing a specialist because of my age (I had just turned thirty-eight when we discovered we were with child), he quickly said no. "Unless you have complications, we don't need to get an outside doctor involved. We won't have any of that," he said.

He made me feel confident that everything was going to be fine, and that helped my faith.

"For we are saved by hope: but hope that is seen is not hope: for what a man seeth, why doth he yet hope for?"

Romans 8:24 (KJV)

Looking back on the four pregnancies we had, I didn't have to do anything but the bare minimum to conceive, but I thought that was all that was required, and for some people, it is. Looking at those around me, it seemed like some of the people I knew and witnessed only had to look at each other, and they were getting pregnant time after time. Granted, I don't know other people's stories unless they share them. But to me, it looked as if it was effortless. For me, even the effort I put it came up short. It felt like some sort of cruel joke. Either I wasn't holding my mouth right or clapping on the right pattern or something. I kept waiting for someone to pop out and announce that I was being punked or something.

One day, while sitting at home minding my business, I received a call from a dear friend who is more like a sister. She asked me in so many words, "What are you doing? Do you guys want to get pregnant or not?" She fussed me out in the most loving, sisterly way, and she said, "You have to know your cycle... when you ovulate and when the peak times are." What in the world? I thought. Why do I have to do all of that if it's God's design for us to have children? He commanded us to be fruitful and multiply, so why do I have to do all that? She said, "Do you want a baby or not?" She gave me recommendations on ovulation apps I could use and a lubricant to buy. I think she just got frustrated, and she just said, "What's your address?"

About a week later, I received a box in the mail addressed to me that had her name on it. I laughed as I opened it and found a big bag of ovulation predictors and a tube of lubricant that helps to make sure the sperm isn't killed before it reaches the egg. There were also pregnancy tests and a note that said, "Now get busy." Ok, so there wasn't an actual note, but that was the sentiment that I got with the box.

You'd have to know this friend to know why she insisted on sending me this care package. She and I grew up a grade apart. When I was in the fifth grade, she was in the fourth, but we are the same age. We are the same age, but she always seemed more mature than I was to me. It was probably because our lives were so different, and we were somewhat sheltered. But I have always looked up to her. She's always been a go-getter, and though she has been through a whole lot, nothing seems to get her down. She makes life look like things are easy. She has always had and still has a determination that I've never personally understood until she called me that day. She left home after she graduated from high school and hasn't looked back since. She's done many great things, including starting a non-profit organization in her city that brings food to children in food deserts via an old school bus that she gutted and repurposed and made into a mobile grocery store of sorts. They deliver food to children so that no child has to go hungry. And that's just one thing. I mean, she's amazing.

She wanted me to experience motherhood so bad that she insisted on sending me a care package with some supplies to "help" me realize my dream. She's always pushed me out of my comfort zone. In college, I experienced my first international flight with her as we boarded a plane and went to Cancún, Mexico for Spring Break. On that trip, I did things I wouldn't have done if she wasn't there. We swam in the ocean and went riding on motor scuba bikes. I literally got to touch beautiful bright colored fish that were only an arm's length, sometimes less, away. If life were a sandbox, I played it safe...she played hard!

Not only did she send me the supplies, but she also called me to make sure I was actually using the supplies she sent me. She knows me well. I always thought I'd always been laid back...or what some would consider laid back. Now I see I was fearful, and that was causing me to wish something would happen without requiring me to take action but that's not faith. Last week, these words came to me: Hope speaks. Faith acts.

Now take a look at this:

Yesterday morning, as I laid in my bed, I looked up the definition of hope. According to Siri, as a noun, hope means a feeling of expectation and desire for a certain thing to happen. As a verb, it means "want something to happen or be the case." Then I asked her to look up faith. As a noun, it means complete confidence or trust in someone or something or a strong belief in God or the doctrines of religion based on spiritual apprehension rather than proof.

Are you as blown away as I am? To me, this shows that hope is a great place to start, but to realize a manifestation of whatever it is you desire, faith—which is action—is necessary. I thought I was operating in faith, but I wasn't. I'm sure you already have this revelation, but just in case you need a little help like I did, you're going to have to take that next step. So, what is the next step for you?

What is it that you are hoping for? Your husband? A successful mentor? A profitable business? Healing? Health? Wealth? Whatever it is, I want to encourage you to go back and take a look at your situation again. Check and see if you are really operating in faith or if you're stuck in hope. I know if it weren't for my dear friends, I probably wouldn't have made a move so urgently. Who knows, maybe later we would've gotten pregnant again, but maybe not. Are you willing to wait and see? Do you have time to waste? Are you really waking by faith? Is there one more step you should take?

Because my friend Lisa did it for me, I am going to take the liberty here and be the push for you that she was for me. The time is NOW! If you've already written your vision and have the expectation that (enter what you are believing or hoping in God for here) will happen, I am lovingly but actively compelling you to take a step of faith. Whatever you need to do to solidify it in the heavenlies and in the earth, do that. I don't know what it is, but I believe you do. You don't have to get anyone's permission or make an announcement or an Instagram post about it—just move. Now, if you need accountability, get it, but don't get stuck waiting for someone to give you permission to go after what God already promised was yours. Move in faith. Let it lead you. It may feel crazy—you may feel crazy doing it, but do it anyway.

I feel like I am speaking in generalities, so let's be specific. Do you need to go look at wedding dresses? Begin planning that conference you feel like you want to host? Go look at houses or buildings? Have you gotten engaged, but you need to take the next step and get married? Maybe you need to write that book that you said you wanted to write years ago but can't quite find the time. What are you waiting for? Go!

When I think about how fortunate I am to have such amazing friends, it makes me smile. I'm humbled. Oftentimes, they believe in me much more than I do. Another friend I met about six or seven years ago over the phone. People say there is no distance in prayer and that God is everywhere, but when I met this powerhouse, I KNEW God is always up to something.

When we met, I was the office manager at a local pediatric therapy company. She and her husband and family lived in China and were possibly moving back stateside to Oklahoma, where my husband and

I live. She was doing research on therapy clinics she could visit while she was in the city, to see which one she wanted to take her son to for an evaluation. She said she did a google search and the clinic where I worked was the first option that came up. So, she called.

On a typical day, I wasn't the one who answered the phone at the clinic, but that day, for some reason, I did. And after speaking with her, I knew it was divine. She and I sat and talked, uninterrupted for about an hour. Now, that uninterrupted part alone was a miracle.

My office was at the front of the clinic, and it was a bit of a Jack and Jill set up, so people would walk through my office all the time to get to the front desk. But on that day, no one walked through there for the entire duration of the call. And when I tell you God moved, I mean He moved! Unbeknownst to me, it was the middle of the night where she was. She shared that she had been praying about which place to visit, and when I answered the phone, she knew God had answered her prayers. I'd also been praying about some things as that job was very stressful. So stressful in fact that I experienced one of my four miscarriages while working there. I was eventually fired from that job, but not before she and I got to meet. Both meeting her and being fired

turned out to be blessings for me.

When she and her family made a visit to Tulsa some months later,

and we finally met, it was as if we'd known each other forever. We

became really good friends. We even worked together at the new

clinic, an audiology clinic I went to work for. We are still friends to

this day. During our tenure together at the audiology clinic, she told

me about a book she'd read entitled Supernatural Childbirth. She

emailed a digital copy to me, which I read and have since forwarded

to many other women. I just searched my email today (9/2019), and it

was January 4, 2012 when she emailed it to me. See it here:

From: Jonnel
Date: Wed, Jan 4, 2012 at 2:51 PM
Subject: Fwd: Supernatural Childbirth
Excellent book!
Tell me what you think

That book literally changed my life. It changed my perspective on

the promises of God and taught me what they were and how to stand on them in prayer. If not for these two dear friends and their assistance, I don't know if I would have had the courage to become the mother of Hope.

Another friend that has been and is a huge joy to our lives is a friend I met in church. I remember our first meeting. I didn't know it then, but it was her very first day at our church. A lady named Ruth (I know... right?!), who I thought was her aunt, introduced us. "I don't know anybody here," she said. "Oh," I replied, and a conversation something like this ensued.

Me: So, what brings you to Tulsa?

Her: I moved here for work.

Me: Oh, where do you work?

Her: I work at ABC company (not actual company name).

Me: Oh! Then you have to meet my husband. He works there, too!

Before I knew it, I was rushing off to find my husband so that I could introduce her to him. Afterward, I thought, you nut...what are you doing? You don't know this lady from a hole in the wall, and you're introducing her to your husband?! I laugh at myself now when I think about it.

Thankfully, everything turned out better than fine, and she became like a sister to me. I have a special affinity for her for many reasons, but one of them is because her name is one of the names my mom considered giving me before she, with the help of one of her dear friends, decided on my name, which she gave me because my dad is a Taurus.

I have so many wonderful memories with this friend. The one that stands out right now is the day I thought I was going to miscarry my now four-year-old daughter. I'd gone to a funeral, and it was a very hot day. I met my parents there, and afterward, we stood outside and chatted like people often do. I don't think I drank enough water that day because when I got home, I began cramping. I went to the bathroom and was astonished to see blood when I wiped. The first thing I did was panic. When you've gone through miscarriage, unless you've had a successful pregnancy with bleeding, the sight of blood is enough to evoke panic. As the book *Supernatural childbirth* says, I learned that when we experience what could be setbacks or receive reports that are contrary to what the word of God says, we have to boldly declare the truth. Remember what the definition of faith was?

a strong belief in God or the doctrines of religion based on spiritual apprehension rather than proof...

So, there may be proof (which is defined as: evidence sufficient to establish a thing as true, or to produce belief in its truth). But proof is not truth. As Believers, we know truth to be what God's word says about a thing. Let me put it this way: seeing blood and having cramps that day could have very well been proof that I was going to miscarry for the fifth time, but I'd prepared myself for the possibility of another setback by gathering, memorizing, and writing some scriptures to use for just this type of situation, so I was able to apply the TRUTH (God's word) to the proof.

Now that all sounds real good, but I am going to keep it real. I was immediately tempted to panic. I spoke the Scripture over myself, but because of my history of miscarriage, I was nearly paralyzed with fear. And I didn't feel strong enough to speak that word and *believe it* on my own. My husband was at work, and I didn't want to bother or worry him or for him to cause me to become hysterical. (He's a laid back person, so I had no doubt he would have attempted to calm me to the best of his ability, but this situation called for something different. I didn't know what it was, but something in my spirit told me she would.) So I reached out for the help of my dear friend, who told me to stay calm, get some cold water, breathe, lie down, and worship.

So that's what I did. I remember it like it was yesterday. After we hung up the phone, I lay down on the couch in my back room, our little dog on the floor by my side, and I began to rub my belly as if to comfort the baby. I began to worship with tears running down my face. Our sweet dog looked on with concern. I assured her I was ok even though I didn't know if I was. As she sat down next to me, I continued to sing. I don't remember which songs I sang, but I remember that a little while later I woke up, cramp-free. I didn't even realize I'd fallen asleep. I got up and went to the bathroom to see if I was still bleeding. When I wiped, there was no blood. I was flooded with relief. I didn't have another experience of that nature for the rest of my pregnancy.

This blessing of a sister, who I am so honored to call my friend, encouraged and calmed me at a very critical point. I was about five or six months pregnant at that point. This was when I realized I had absolutely no control other than the control I had over my thoughts. Initially, when I began to bleed, I considered calling my doctor to see if he could do anything, but the moment I picked up the phone, the thought occurred to me that there was nothing he would be able to do for me. There is no magic pill you can take to prevent miscarriage. Often, they say that once it starts, you just have to let it take its course because the body knows what it's doing. For the cases where the cervix is not strong enough to hold the baby, there is a surgical procedure that can be done, but that wasn't my case. I didn't even know if my situation would qualify me as a candidate for it. This is the moment I *knew* that if I was going to make it through this pregnancy with a healthy baby (as had been one of my declarations), I was completely reliant on God. So I told Him, Lord, You are the *only* one who can get me through this alive. My doctor can't do it. My husband can't help me. My mom and dad can't help me....only You can make me a joyful mother of children. I am *depending* on You. I know it's Your will for me to be fruitful and multiply. You commanded it. You thought this whole thing up. I know you can do this, so please, *please* bring us out for Your glory. I will give you all of the praise, and I thank you in advance for doing it according to your Word. I believe You can, and I believe You will.

I am here today, and I am so glad to say He did. And He is no respecter of persons (Acts 10:34). If He did it for me, He will do it for you. But *you* are going to have to dig in and fight. By fight I mean stand on the Word of God and don't let go until you see what you have been asking and believing for. Take charge of your thoughts and focus on the outcome you want to see.

He's faithful to do it if you're crazy enough to believe it and apply the word to it.

CHAPTER 5 - WHEN HOPE SPEAKS

"Hope deferred makes the heart sick,

but a longing fulfilled is a tree of life."

Proverbs 13:12

Hope (our daughter) has brightened my days and filled my heart in a way that I never dreamed possible. I can imagine that the way I feel about her is how God feels about me and you. I feel a great sense of responsibility to and for her... to nurture her and build her up; to make sure she knows she is thoroughly loved and to make sure she feels protected and encouraged. I want to do everything I can to make sure each and every day I get to spend with her is special.

If I can be honest, she has probably encouraged me much more than I have encouraged her. My dad tells me that I was a lot like her as a child, only a little more laid back. Her freedom and carefreeness feel familiar to me. At some point in my adulthood, I feel like I lost touch with it...and myself. She puts me back in touch with the little girl I was and all the big dreams I had. She causes me to dream new dreams and push past my comfort zone to try and create a reality for her that I only dream of. There's that word again. Dream. It blows my mind to think she was a dream, and now she is a walking, talking reality. I'm in tears thinking about how totally awesome God is... that He, Who created this entire universe, would choose to collaborate with us, with *ME,* to bring forth His most prized creation is unfathomable and indescribably humbling. I garner a greater understanding of the love God has for me from interacting with and watching her. She says some of the most profound things at the most unexpected times.

Most recently, while she and I were shopping in our favorite grocery store, I was thinking about what to get for dinner. My mind was simultaneously bombarded with worries about money. I'd recently left my job at a financial services firm, and my husband had been going through some health issues that caused him to stop working. We'd liquidated all of his retirement and our savings to try and make ends meet, and I was at a loss for what to do—so I guess I had a lot on my mind. As I was walking down the aisle of the supermarket, I let out a big sigh. "Lord!" I exclaimed. Apparently, I'd done it more than once without realizing it because she sweetly asked me, "Mommy, why do you keep saying that?" Not knowing I'd said it before, I asked, "Saying what?" "Lord," she said. "Why do you keep saying that?" As I thought to myself, I hesitantly answered, "I guess it's a cry to Him for help. I need help."

"Mommy, you don't have to cry for help," she said. "All you have to do is ask the king and say, 'Oh, great King, please help me,' and he will." Where she got that from, I have no idea, but she surely said the right thing at the right time.

It was so simple, yet I hadn't even thought of just asking God for help. The three-year-old me would've probably gotten it, but the forty-two-year-old me thought, wow. Why didn't I think of that, and how does she even know? I was sure she and I might have been talking about two totally different things, but deep down, I feel intuitively that she knows exactly what she said. What I don't know is if she knows how it impacted me.

Many times I find myself at the point of tears inspired by the insight I receive from this pint-sized sage. Because of her, I am inspired to go back and pick up the dreams that I left behind out of hopelessness or overwhelm or fear. Her mere presence has invoked me to prayer and praise more times than I can admit. Prayer about any and everything I can think of... little things that I feel silly praying about and big things that I feel silly praying about. If I look back, I can see how this entire journey, from losing four pregnancies to having our daughter, has invoked me to prayer. I don't think I'd pray like I do now if she weren't here.

I was so hopeless and angry and defeated before she came. I didn't think I would ever get to realize this dream I now write about that has become my reality.

And isn't that how life is with a lot of things? Do we ever really know if we will be able to fulfill the goals and plans we have for ourselves? No. We *hope* we will be able to, but we never know if we will. I'm so grateful that I was able to experience this miracle firsthand, and I am so grateful to be sharing this experience with you.

I need you to know that though your road may be different than mine, I know how it feels to walk a lonely road. A road paved with questions and no answers. Time and time again, I asked God why am I going through this? Perhaps it was for you?

If you are reading this and you're at the point of desperation and weariness, I want you to know you are at the right place for hope to speak.

Believe it or not, it has not been easy writing this book. It has been emotionally and mentally challenging. I've felt resistance, mostly internally. I've been proudly sharing with people that I am writing a book about my journey to motherhood, but for some reason, there were weeks, months even, when I did everything *but* write. Maybe it was some sort of self-sabotage tactic, or, as my sister, Melycia put it, a hesitancy to reopen the wounds.. I don't know. All I know is I hope and pray the words that are on these pages are able to encourage and galvanize someone to believe for the things that are in their heart. Go back and look again. If there's something, a desire, that's burning in you to be or do or have something that has been calling out to you, I want to encourage... no, assert, rather compel you to dust it off, put it back on your prayer list and begin to move back toward it. Pursue it passionately. It ain't over until it's over!

I wonder if people know that you never forget the pregnancies you lost; or the possibilities that could have been. After we had our daughter, I prayed that God would never let me forget how I felt while I was going through the process. I don't ever want to forget the disappointment, the anger, the questions I had. That big mess of emotions and experiences translates to quite a message, or so I've heard.

I used to struggle thinking the dreams I desired were contrary to the will of God if they were enjoyable to me. It seemed too easy. I reasoned that His work and desire for me had to be something I'd only do if He dragged me kicking and screaming. Thank heavens someone told me the gifts God has given us are indications and clues as to what

He has for us and they are oftentimes things we enjoy or have a knack for. I'm so glad.

If you're unsure, keep bringing that thing, your promise, up before God. He delights in blessing us, His children. He wants to see us blessed. "He has a plan for us; to give us hope and a future." (Jeremiah 29:11) I used to hear my former pastor say, "Don't be afraid to hold on to the horns of the altar." If Jacob wrestled with God we can too. Don't let go until you get your answer.

So... what should you do now? Good question. I don't know, but I'll bet you do. What I do know is where you are is right where you are supposed to be. See, when I suffered loss after loss, it brought me to a place where I had a lot of questions. (Lord, was it something I did? Was there something you told me to do that I didn't do? Is it a generational curse? Did I open some door that I shouldn't have? Did I go left when You said go right? Is there unconfessed sin? Maybe an attitude of heart that needs to be corrected? Am I harboring unforgiveness? What is it?!!!! Why am I going through this?)

I heard someone say the other day that some people are going through the fire just so they can share with someone else, after they've come through it, how God brought them out. Maybe your test is to produce your yes and a stronger prayer habit?

When I was in North Carolina in May of 2015 with my two best friends and my mom, we were at a prayer breakfast, and the hostess, whose house we were in, prayed and spoke a prophetic word over each of us. When she got to me, she said, "I see that you get pregnant, and then it goes away and again and again..." She said, "I hear The Lord say there's nothing physically wrong with you. What you have is a faith issue." Can I be honest? I was absolutely and utterly offended. I didn't tell her that, but after I got home, I asked God. What is she talking about? A faith issue? I know who You are. I have faith. I believe. But when it came down to it, I didn't have faith that God would do it for ME! And I wasn't familiar enough with the promises of God concerning childbirth to be able to effect change in my situation.

And by searching The Word and being in constant communication with Him through prayer, I found that out. And I am glad I did. So...

what is it for you?

I feel like that is part of what it means when the Bible says in Hosea 4:6 that "my people are destroyed for lack of knowledge." This is why it's not just enough to hear the word, but we have to know it for ourselves. No one else on the face of the earth could have dug into the Word of God and searched out the promises concerning my situation and believed and countered the attacks of the enemy with His word but me. Now it's your turn to do it for you. When hope speaks faith acts.

HOPE REIGNS - DECLARATIONS/SCRIPTURES

"As for me, I will always have hope;

I will praise you more and more."

Psalms 71:14

On Mother's Day this year as I found myself trying to help my spunky, bubbly, loving, four-year-old, daughter don her swimsuit after what can only be described as an all-out meltdown following a conversation with her daddy about what she wanted to wear to go out and get me Mother's Day breakfast, I was reminded how just five years ago, this day was bitter for me. I didn't know just two short weeks from this day, five years ago, I would conceive that fiery four-year-old and life would never be the same.

Let me set the scene. It was Mother's Day of May 2015. In years prior to this, I had silently suffered four pregnancy losses. So, going to church or even out on Mother's Day, I had to prepare myself for the influx of what people thought were well wishes. "Happy Mother's Day," they would say, and then they realized I had no children. I would smile and pray tears didn't fall as I tried to make my way to the door before anyone else tried to start the process all over again. Today, five years ago was hard. So, I know how it feels to have always wanted a child—or, in my case, to really start wanting it when it felt like everything in the earth was telling you you couldn't or wouldn't be able to. I know how it feels to be invited to baby shower after baby shower with a smile on your face and joy in your heart for the mother-to-be, but to feel like you were dying inside from barrenness. Now I know how Hannah and Sarah must have felt.

If you are reading this, maybe you have experienced something similar? Perhaps you have a loved one who has? Perhaps you are the spouse or partner of someone who has gone through recurrent pregnancy loss or the loss of a child after childbirth, and you feel just as disappointed and hurt as they do. Because we don't wear badges, like scarlet letters, that announce how many pregnancies, full-term or not, we have endured, I recommend that you do what I experienced this year. I told a Facebook friend, who I really don't know personally "Happy Mother's Day," and she simply responded with "XOXO."

She, not knowing my backstory, didn't echo the same sentiment back to me, and though some may find it strange, I found it refreshing. You see, after experiencing year after year with loss after loss, a day like Mother's Day can be a very hard and bittersweet day for women and for the men who love them. Though my husband and I now have a healthy preschooler, I will never forget the road we walked to get here.

If you still desire to have children, I want to offer some declarations that may be of assistance.

Declarations

I f you have endured multiple pregnancy losses, you may be gun shy or hesitant to rejoice when you get a positive pregnancy test, like I was. I was so grateful to have been introduced to *Supernatural Childbirth by Jackie Mize*. I credit it for helping me to locate, recognize, know, and be able to stand on the promises of God for my blessing.

It had, and suggested the reader have, clear declarations from The Bible to combat any opposition to the fulfillment of the promise (doubt, fear, etc.) that may try to arise unsuspectingly. If you haven't heard of it or read it you can buy it on Amazon. It was also one of my baby shower gifts by a sweet coworker who had no clue that I'd read it.

I've heard it said that faith is a muscle. To be built, it must be exercised (or worked out). So that lets me know to strengthen it—our faith will be tested. Your road may not be easy, but if there are challenges, know they are opportunities to stand on the faith that we profess. Inspired by *Supernatural Childbirth*, I created a few custom declarations based in and on the word of God that I spoke over myself and our daughter to keep myself encouraged when I was tempted to doubt or operate in fear. Some of them were just me adding my name where the scripture said her or him or man or woman.

What is a declaration? According to dictionary.com, it is a noun that means a formal or explicit statement or announcement or the formal announcement of the beginning of a state or condition.

Synonyms include: affirmation, proclamation, and revelation.

Here's an example:

"He maketh the barren woman to keep house, and to be a joyful mother of children. Praise ye the Lord!" Psalms 113:9 (KJV)

Here's my declaration: I am a joyful mother of children. Praise ye the Lord!

- I am the head and not the tail, above only and not beneath. God is for me and with me, and I cannot fail.

Here's another one. This is the scripture:

"For I know the plans I have for you," declares the Lord, "plans to prosper you and not to harm you, plans to give you hope and a future." Jeremiah 29:11 (NIV)

- God has plans to prosper me, and not to harm me...plans to give me hope and a future!

One more:

- I am fruitful in everything I do. Everything I touch and all that I do produces good fruit. Where I am, fruitfulness follows.
- Today, I will partner with God to produce miracles. I am a

miracle, and I produce miracles.

- I am at peace, I live peaceably, and I produce peace.

Now it's your turn.

Based on the scriptures you have located, what declarations can you create to help you speak your world into existence and support your stance of faith and hope?

- _____
  _____
  _____
  _____
  _____

- _____
  _____
  _____
  _____
  _____

- _____
  _____
  _____
  _____
  _____

- _____
  _____
  _____
  _____

- _____
  _____
  _____
  _____

- _____
  _____
  _____
  _____

- _____

_____

_____

_____

No matter what happens, remember you are not alone. God is with you.

Scriptures

I'd like to share a few of the scriptures that helped me during my journey and that I still use today.

Isaiah 40:31 (NIV) "They That Wait Upon The Lord, Shall Renew Their Strength, They Shall Mount Up with Wings of Eagles, They Shall Run and Not Be Weary Walk and not Faint."

Hebrews 10:23 (KJV) "Let us hold fast the profession of our faith without wavering; (for he is faithful that promised;)"

Hebrews 10:23 (ASV) "Let us hold fast the confession of our hope that it waver not; for he is faithful that promised."

Speaking of faith, check this out:

Hebrews 11:1-6 (KJV) "Now faith is the substance of things hoped for, the evidence of things not seen. For by it the elders obtained a good report. Through faith we understand that the worlds were framed by the word of God, so that things which are seen were not made of things which do appear."

I just want to pause right here...so in verse one, we learn that faith is the stuff that things we hope for are made of...the evidence of things not seen. Now, go down to verse three. This is so key to me. Remember, I am not a theologian, nor did I go to seminary. But to me, verse three is SO important because we see the framework for how God created all that we now see that we feel has always been there. What does it say? Oops...that's a hint I didn't mean to give. It says, "the worlds were framed by the WORD of God."

So, that says to me that I shouldn't expect to see it right off. What is "it?" It is the blessing of being a mother or a strong marriage or that job that you feel you want or whatever else it is that you feel God put on your heart to be/do/have. It says to me, though I can't see it, what I CAN do is frame my world by what I say. That's so important to me because I used to be one of those people who would pride myself on telling it "like it is." But, what does God's word say? We are not called to tell it like it is...we tell it like we want it to be. For the world seeing is believing. For us believing is seeing, and that's not just a Christian principle. It's scientific, but that's a whole other book.

- *Romans 4:17 (KJV) says it like this: "(as it is written: "I have made thee a father of many nations"), in the presence of Him whom he believed, even God, who quickeneth the dead and calleth those things which are not, as though they were."*

- *I like this version: Romans 4:17 (AMPC) "As it is written, I have made you the father of many nations. [He was appointed our father] in the sight of God in Whom he believed, Who gives life to the dead and speaks of the nonexistent things that [He has foretold and promised] as if they [already] existed."*

So, when I was laying on my couch one day at nearly five months pregnant, bleeding and cramping and scared I was going to miscarry yet again, I had to say what The Word of God says over my situation not what I saw or felt because, like my Pastor said today in her message, "Your situation—our situations—have ears, and they are listening for our direction and are subject to our command."

These declarations are so that you have an arrow in your quiver, so to speak, to shoot at any force that would come to try to steal your promise.

Here's another one I refer to:

- In addition to all this, take up the shield of faith, with which you can extinguish all the flaming arrows of the evil one. That is Ephesians 6:16 NIV. Read the entire chapter. Pay special attention starting at verse eleven. It talks about putting on the armor of God, and it is so good.

Ahhh. Here's another one that helped (helps) me to make sure I am not fighting my spouse or my boss or my body or whatever other natural opposition may present itself. Your fight—our fight—is not a natural fight. As believers, we know we are warring with things that are otherworldly, so we have to make sure our weapons are not of this world, or they won't be effective in lending us victory.

- *Ephesians 6:12 (NKJV)*

  "For we do not wrestle against flesh and blood, but against the rulers, against the authorities, against the cosmic powers over this present darkness, against the spiritual forces of evil in the heavenly places."

- *1 Peter 5:8 (NKJV)*

  "Be sober, be vigilant; because your adversary the devil, as a roaring lion, walketh about, seeking whom he may devour."

- *Ezekiel 37:4 (NIV)*

  "Then he said to me, "Prophesy to these bones and say to them, 'Dry bones, hear the word of the Lord!'"

- *2 Timothy 1:7 (KJV)*

  "For God hath not given us the spirit of fear; but of power, and of love, and of a sound mind."

- *Proverbs 18:10 (KJV)*

  "The name of the Lord is a strong tower; the righteous runneth into it, and is safe."

- *Numbers 23:19 (KJV)*

  "God is not a man, that he should lie; neither the son of man, that he should repent: hath he said, and shall he not do it? or hath he spoken, and shall he not make it good?"

- *Matthew 19:26 (KJV)*

  "But Jesus beheld them, and said unto them, With men this is impossible; but with God all things are possible."

- *Mark 9:23 (KJV)*

  "Jesus said unto him, If thou canst believe, all things are possible to him that believeth."

- *Isaiah 26:3 (AMP)*

  "You will keep in perfect and constant peace the one whose mind is steadfast [that is, committed and focused on you—in both inclination and character], Because he trusts and takes refuge in You [with hope and confident expectation]."

- *I John 5:4 (KJV)*

  For whosoever is born of God overcometh the world. And this is the victory that overcometh the world, even our faith.

- *Psalm 128:3 (NKJV)*

  "Your wife will be like a fruitful vine within your house; your children will be like olive shoots around your table."

- *Exodus 23:26 (NLT)*

  "There will be no miscarriages or infertility in your land, and I will give you long, full lives."

ACKNOWLEDGMENTS

Meagan, I still remember that day at my dining room table where you, Andrea and I prayed and talked about our hopes and dreams. And to see them manifest. Wow! Only God! (Andrea, now it's your turn—wink!)

Special thanks go to my family:

To my husband, Anthony, for agreeing that I should record this account and for supporting and encouraging me along the way and also for sharing your side of our story. Thank you for being the man I prayed for, who loves me like Christ, loves the church, even and especially when I am difficult to love.

Momma and Daddy, you are the best parents ever. I am so blessed God chose you to bring me about. Daily, I am amazed at your love for me. I really don't know if I'll ever be able to comprehend it.

To my two sisters, Melycia and Audra, also known as two-thirds of the "Girly Girls," y'all are my day ones. Through ups and downs, we three shall be. Love you both.

To my church family, a huge thank you for your love, prayers, and support. It has meant and means the world to Anthony and I.

Thanks also to my friends, who are as much a part of my family as my blood. I have the *best* two best friends anyone could ask for (Tori and Dége). Y'all get me! To the whole host of other girlfriends and cousins who are like sisters, you ladies are the wind beneath my wings. I stand on your shoulders. If I named you all, I would surely forget someone and that I don't want to do. If you are reading this and feel I may be talking about you, I am. Many times it was your voices that I heard telling me not to give up. It was your hands I held and your shoulders I cried on. Words can't express my gratitude.

My Asha, you are an answered prayer and a manifested miracle. I am tremendously humbled to have had the privilege to bring your life forth into this earth. In reality, you gave birth to me. You said it once, and at first, I didn't understand, but now I get it. Yes, sweetheart, when you were born, *I* was born. I love you SOOOOO much. To God be all the glory!

Lastly, to the men and women who will turn these pages, I want to say thank you.

FRAMING HOPE

Here I am a young girl, about 13 years old or so.

Anthony and I on our wedding day just after we had been pronounced man and wife in October of 2007.

My beloved friend, Lisa, who sent me the care package.

Here we are, at our baby reveal, with my sweet friend Tamarra, who was the medical assistant at our second doctor's office.

At her Baby Dedication ceremony in October 2017

Asha and I at her first quinceañera. It was her first time meeting a "real-life princess", as she put it.

Auntie Mary, Uncle Bee, Bear, Daddy and Me

ABOUT THE AUTHOR

Tara Payne lives in Tulsa, Oklahoma, along with her husband, their daughter, and their loyal sidekick, a lovable mixed-breed rescue named Teagan. Recently, she left a career in financial services behind in favor of pursuing her lifelong passion of being a full-time creative, entrepreneur, writer, speaker, and published author. When she isn't writing, you might find Tara singing on the worship team at the church she attends, writing poetry, cooking, creating impromptu songs and dances with her daughter, or exploring the city, always with a pen and pad in her hand.

Made in the USA
Columbia, SC
29 September 2020